STILL DIRTY

POEMS 2009-15

∞

COMMUNE EDITIONS

Red Epic, Joshua Clover
We Are Nothing and So Can You, Jasper Bernes
That Winter the Wolf Came, Juliana Spahr

A Series of Un/Natural/Disasters, Cheena Marie Lo
Still Dirty: Poems 2009-2015, David Lau

Still Dirty

DAVID LAU

∞

Commune Editions
Oakland, California
communeeditions.com

An imprint of AK Press / AK Press UK
Oakland, California (akpress@akpress.org)
Edinburgh, Scotland (ak@akedin.demon.co.uk)

Commune Editions design by Front Group Design
(frontgroupdesign.com)
Cover illustration by Amze Emmons

Library of Congress Cataloging-in-Publication Data 2015959374

Lau, David
Still Dirty: Poems 2009-2015 / David Lau

ISBN 9781934639184 (pbk.: alk. paper)

Printed on acid-free paper by McNaughton & Gunn, Michigan, U.S.A. The
paper used in this publication meets the minimum requirements of ANSI/
NISO Z39.48-1992 (R2009)(*Permanence of Paper*).

FOR LAURA AND CARLOS

TABLE OF CONTENTS

I

Money Shot Through Glass Crane Floor 3

Tiqqun Style 5

Communism Today 7

Neanderthal Street Journal 10

There Should Be Like a Really Interesting Political Discussion… 11

Re: FWD: Is this List Still Active? 12

Time in the Novel 14

An Indication of Guerrilla Activity Undertaken 16

Beater Pride of Lions 17

Bad Opposites 18

Recycled, Lucky 20

No Movies 21

Near Earth Object 22

II

Curtain Design for Victory over the Sun 25

Ghost Factory 26

My Breast Is Swarming with Restless Waves 27

In the Lower World's Tiniest Grains 29

Eyebrow of Jungle 30

Gun Show   31
From the Kola Peninsula to Lake Baikal   32
On the Path   33
Flesh-Colored Shirt   34
Fleur de De La Soul   35
Lumumba Zapata College   37
Gloriae   38

III

Make a Problem   41
Still Dirty (Subclip)   42
How to Win a Strike (the Phantom Menace)   43
Curtain Design for Victory over the Sun   45
What is the Car Movement Like?   46
Star Nemesis   47
Vigilantopolis   48
Tombs Called Mathilde   49
Linati Schema (feat. Laetitia Sadier)   50
Bassnectar Is Playing D Lot on Friday   51
Short Talk about Freud   52
Todos Los Everything   53
Shaniqwa   54
The Trumpet Blacks   55

IV

Moreno Valley, Trapezoid of Light   59
The Triple-Double Dream of Spring   60
Pythian   62
Panegyric   63
Garbage Collectors   64
Resource Optimization   65
Source   66
The Three Wants   67
Dialectic in a Barbaric Bog   68
Literary Critics Have Confused Aesthetics   69

Poem   70

Summer Rains   72

Skid Row-kyo   74

Like a Storm System of Post-QE Emerging Market Bubbles   78

Acknowledgments   80

I.

Money Shot Through Glass Crane Floor

Electro riot tonight, May Day, Santa Cruz.
The windows of Urban Outfitters were smashed
after Hova's song about New York came on
the skateboard driven PA.
Nobody looted a thing.
(A few months later
hella goodbye Oakland Foot Locker.)

The crowd's fissiparous dissolution came
as it neared the clock tower
and we wound up at the Red Room.
Liv was pissed. I don't remember anyone
saying, "When the jewelry place
went down our Justice song was on."

We had numbers. The homie Pat broke
up some fights. Don was there.
Homie'd been quoted in the *Times*.
Bonnano (in a cheap suit), Maya,
and I walked together, hurried (better),
as the black flag went up over the action.
Jo told me she didn't want to get arrested.
When the bouncers at Motiv dragged Sam down,
a masked groupuscule freed him up.

3

Back at the neon red debrief nobody said much.
"We crossed this Burmese river" or
"The Punjab is a land with five rivers."
I drank from a glass of beer and remembered
the Alexander Kluge VHS
The Eiffel Tower, King Kong, and the White Woman.
The wind was blowing down trees;
at the port of Long Beach,
a Mitsubishi crane un-stacked
a glow-blue sheet of wind.
I've been rolling around with a bunch of Fleetwood Macks.
We are the crisis.

Tiqqun Style

Crave you *Exarchia* chromed up with *Koukouloforoi*?
Syntagma sipping on slurry?
Do you like banks?
Neither contest nor demand constitute force.
Prisoners or farmers. No flaneur.
(Lost this precarity
given newfangled "security.") Don't desertify,
don't propagate liberalism
with the urgency audible to power.
Dodge fares, steal / practice escape.
Seed trade the total submission called legal.
Communize the simple lands of the old world.
Crave you the subject / simultaneity early and lake.
Time ceased waiting life linked thought.
Give up desires without intensity, democracy.
Crave you sectarianism, particular truth.
Not afraid / forming gangs—we are
what has cubicle isolation,
squat scene, criminal origins,
field work, 80s purge.
Scrape out the inside, the false differences,
flight facilities. (Exhaustion.) Don't give in.
We are in a civil war, irremediably there.
Multiply and consolidate the fly artwork.

5

Deep cogitations then sleep.
Normality subsidized this lingo.
In London police struck and nearly killed
a young man called Alfie—dripping in gold.

Communism Today

1

Call-in request line binding force
cut back, fought
with Mozart and the percussion great
called Non-Los Angeles.
They came around the

building with our comrades
in front of them as shields.
Fuck Dave Kliger.
Which one of these anarchist faggots stole my SIM card?
See if the janitor has the key to open these doors.

He's the person we need everything.
The telos today closer to undead,
insurrectionary Velazquezes incapable
of enduring independent labor monitors—
wild Mike is straight up drugs.

Sri Lankan and subjective confusions
adopted that language
as in Balzac when rude boys
had rivers to cross.
A snort of laughter to knot

en El Encanto Sanitarium
near the freeway river flowing 100,000 stanzas,
let Placitas bloom 1,000 at a time
quickly into inauspicious jobs.
Occupy everything, including Humanities

2

Moody's ratings vultures have no process for light picnic table,
but they do bring chemical

sprays to The City of London, humid with so little high morale,
such a limited call-up of man.

The time window
in the dime bag

near our distant sun
of fungal alphabets,

papeles for horses.
Roll out the analysis of the base on

a turquoise Ho Chi Minh
hard by the pachyderm

bobcat of bridge. The tossed
office goes down, riverine

in the peculiar behavior of exponents.
We totally had a flier for this one

3

unlike the Mrak Hall walking style

of Kresge's Pomo Afro Homos
hard by the triangular,
                                    submerged
water fountain.
                    Tap rooted
tandoori shore
                    flickers with shelter
beneath the sandwich cart,
fermented chile bean paste twilight.

Guns out with these gents,
Carter and Huggins,
                        Oscar Grant.
The movement ends ICE raids.
Takes places.

4

We're just back from a lawless area
in the south of the country called Irvine,
determined by valleys of the Irrawaddy.
Is anyone worth poisoning?

Which one of us will be the elf king?
I'm just chilling

with several distinct calls, "boom,"
"olive wood," and "delirium."

Torches and tire fires "boom" the movement,
cross out the movement to move.

Neanderthal Street Journal

The film made
me (ninja sonic street carnage)
strangle a mountain ox with my bare hands.
I'm not a tigress like Angelina.
Of course, people want me to be.
But I want to be the contradiction.

There Should Be Like a Really Interesting Political Discussion About Trying to Represent Events When We Have No Access to Them

Thus the groove meme insurgency people,
hood-ass Grandma goodbyes.
I went back to work in the fields again
after eleven years of surgery.
When I left, the long summer died in unison playing,
Madagascar/Spain in the rain's warm pomegranate power lines
y una mini-van airbrushed with a scene of wild dogs.

Re: Fwd: Is This List Still Active

Titties, one two raw, dude, that poem.
Reforma Avenue. Glaciology's last few
advancing glaciers. *Huelga del cobre*
light in the teargas cloud.

Ah, brief were the days of Chilean expropriation.
El ejercito del pueblo and some such *golpista*
in the occluded dialectical revelation
arrow through the boogie. Just water the smudge.

Someday later some will ask us
where we got our style from. From Tokyo's
cesium hotspots down with messy
in differing difference.

I have grown two faces out
the side of my head.
I am the occupation
of Bataille cuerpos mas puerco.

Wasps in the weed smoke,
rainwater river ocean streak blue sun.
Solar Amphipolis.
The privative prefix, that princeling.

Systematic a-systematicity burgeons
with hotties in the struggle
who learn to set bones.
Revenue resulting from exchange,

Morelia Marxista conocido.
An Egyptian dimension
of the Twitter-scape
vanquished all amigos.

Time in the Novel

The relentless disclosure of products thought picture
about the size of reform school,
and much deployed in Ceylon
after a night of delirium and spiritual essences,
like our sixth-month-long
tour in confiscated vehicles from Culiacán:

Skull Bear's right-handedness on the flute
planted blooms every night in a manic,
shrewlike evolution. Phyletic,
like large fossil bones in Argentina, spiky,
percussive, as with Charles Lloyd
in the Soviet Union, he
warned but as waning women
with a biogeography like brissant
knowledge of the black arts
and Meyer Schapiro in *Marxist Quarterly*.

Living things over time tend—the site?—
Acousticlandia? Arabidopsis
made the trip in the recent independence
of consequence, alleles reanneal the seam,
stabilizing directions of diversified antlers

in the painting school, a whale-in-you force,
haplodiploidy like honeycreepers in a fly's…

About the student situation in Greece:
sundownese paper bag huffing out front the ITT school.
Bondholders get a chemical fire.
The plum flower fist association
was recognized by a pig.
Once it becomes a wren-angel-hydra-
Metazoa, mixological, deep down drone weapon,
its distance methods
will decapitate enemies.

An Indication of Guerrilla Activity Undertaken

Knew then we would be going on a long trip.
Nieuw: prepaid ration
for the baroque bioscoop, a lion

on screen, *pas de stars* as though
by an invisible hand unclothed.
This time the number of motion

in relation to a before after. Pain. Full.
Chihuahuan — Sierran — Himalayan and
the friendly Miroslav Hernandez

jackhammered the bells
truth maniac American
people's tribunal for Tlatelelco

housing complex. The vortex/vector
tastes for
THE CHICANO MORATORIUM AGAINST THE VIETNAM WAR.

Beater Pride of Lions

Coconut and Machete
begin a slow class
analysis of Guyanese Society
or when conquest scrambles its jets
("We'll be in Africa in under 10 minutes")

now leaving the Gulf Cartel's main plaza in
the baroque complex of governmental nepotism.
Every man a mad king. Job
interviewization, debt—forced into it, to sell
chant down slavery a keyboard milk.

Bad Opposites

I have presorted
choruses at a special discount window
beneath "wild justice." Do right.
Blue corn fungus light at night
above Managua. Cleared, there has been
a rev up here in the smoking remains
of our camp. It shook still
in the Orfeo. We're overrun,
become reams of vanished atoms: presente!
the urethra, one hurricane,
a terror of wide ski runs
gone all gray through the rocky passage below us…

That camera has been through some wars
with the Amerindian words *Mitla* and *tianguis*,
themselves blown orange flakes
against a bright blue wall,
in Solentiname painting style, a hag
and brutal, pixilated stop now gone.
Help us get these folks off the ground.
We shadow the auto show
near the semi-refulgent attachment
of Michael Jackson. Across the way, past dull
meadow / parking lot

of half-battered punch
clocks and a stack of battle resolve
for the widening, deepening frontline —
that go on *no pasarán non-pavanne*
at the end of the film version of *The Society of the Spectacle*
when an enormous number of people
sit on the floor together in a room. Some stand.
The form of the workers' council gone.
Discord and attrition after dinner
at Forward Observation Post ManBearPig.
Dogs' anger in the autolysis catalyst.
                                    (After the side
knifing, I'm battered and in a pinch.)

Fight the infidel, my beguiling not-goon.
They're coming for you — *fire-ball-destroyed,*
standing-firm-until-this-one-time — Marjah.

Recycled, Lucky

We set up roadblocks with concrete fragments
and our dead.
 We said every other thing in
the expressive aphasia of big capital,

that, "Look,
 I have your película,
the surface
of the hard nut.

(*Nomina sunt odiosa.*) And because

Salome was the mental states of her conspecifics

the insignificance of most suicides
mouthed mountain-rose ice.

Later I logged off at SoundCloud."

No Movies

Mobile web motherfucking street party
another attack today

fight like an Egyptian

in Chicano cinema
mouth taped shut
gun taped to your hand

"The Border Patrol swallows
as many shadows as it can."

She had twenty children, Iztapalapa,
hijos de la chingada

it is accomplished
these streets are full

ghosts hella lay book on fools
who come hang out

Near Earth Object

The bottle-rack-as-hedgehog
funk joint's to stay for good. Name? Hipólito
plays the ultimately determining crescendo
during the guitar solo
of Chicanismo.

The change in ocean scavenges the sweeping,
formidable creature
of return, exoskeleton
of escaped
hatred and surf,

fire goddess of the lotus
just kind of bacon ranch in certain ways…
and light beams checkered like us
unearth clay pots
in the helicopter moon.

Rosa Clará from the forward nectar plane —
there parted the polka
that sustains, broken,
the Whitney's vivid shorthand
of the operation. Catheter

whose beams canceled
black blankets on the river-green arroyo—
there the daily
passage through the wards
magicked up the Triaxium novissimi.

The grotto hated our captors,
sex panthers came on the scene.
The acid differed in the base:
muscle, nerve, viscera, purely immediate.
We mimicked a transition force's vortex of animals.

Quench lost the rise,
lower heat, the different
colored flames like lilies
in the pilaster and quartzite head of a god
on a new plinth for nothing.

I allowed it to went / the heat of an enormous sun
does not stay the same in this room
or the next's music of smoke signaling blanket.
A solvent purified the start.
And then it breaks off everywhere yet

in so far as we are residential
with light, with the years near Año Nuevo
enthroned in the drill bit meant for your skull,
we are a federation of insufficiently musical warriors,
local the 1960s in recycled hand signals;

or it is all continuously happening, a live process
recombined with the vertical interruption
of flashback sequences of the shipwreck
when we win their hearts with an orchid
map that stays for good.

II.

Curtain Design for Victory over the Sun

The universal empire of crime,
      that faggot angel, whether to war on, according—

nears the end of a new period—
      the nunca flamingo in smoke white hedges—

period in which the design ambush
      at the torch indentation
            was known ahead of time by Sun Ra,

that noise of time through Armenia
      (where records indicate you going),
            but less obtuser, the kabobs in neon—redo—

and nothing would anymore be said about
      the protest of heaven, the part
            about police violating the university's autonomy,

because there exist, after all, limits,
      book people for a leftish song,
            limits to the effective—

—lowest, floweriest—channeling of real life.
      Deer hunt a pavilion zone.

Ghost Factory

and feces smear misted by morgue juice,
the sludge of plata o plomo. Tonight
le sinthome sports combat boots
matched with total awareness.
My Post-Employment Benefits Recommendations Update
includes dinner with her.
But who wants to live here
with a left-wing Communist English Instructor?

I was in Cuba once, no I wasn't, yes I was
a simple phone call that is available 24/7
in the 150 language macaronic
enigma-twilight of the Iraq occupation.
Sounds like the underground comet
used to manufacture clear plastic
for minimum security prison microwaves.
San Gabriel River jetty cloud break,
January tides gone sky.

My Breast Is Swarming with Restless Waves

"Of man's first five year plan
at the great end period
shadow on an Aiwa stereo
thought clips
find a tag singly shaggy
and after
from the crew

Gli Apostoli

that sweep winds across
marauders
I am as pleased

crossover
Migra dynamite
the earth shakes fire
What is its name thinking / the stall switch
our desperate generation's iron
the effect of wondering where the sense simply begins and
(*noise: pension fund undermined*)

Las Mujeres de Lima blast offstage
They own factories or something Fidelio

pensive like loyal suicide—unwritten
    total Shakespeare Godard (go die
    imperialist encore),"
    warbled Arrezo, in
        the fight to produce
    hexachord gamut of Guido-like Solfege
    Saracen Zarzuela genre of jets
      who never experienced certain things
<u>Action & Pamphlet</u>   the rock song beneath Vendetta

In the Lower World's Tiniest Grains

There was, I was try…
the Burkeanism of that guy,
the Tennis-Court-Oathification stripe of a leopard sky.

"The fruit that exists in every way is a kind of sandal.
Refulgent with afters wildly reaching is open."

And they fought very hard
to kill (plural)
people in Khost with Dark Star,
the LA variety.
These guys stick maneuver

on you
("That's what we do.")

Line shatters dealings, virtues,
traders, treasures, comers, buyers, lovers,
mergers, justice, court, balance, weight—

the seal absorbs us.

Eyebrow of Jungle

in celebration of a forgotten strike
the ice hotel isn't cold enough

in the laconic mode of a screenplay

here I am

las mujeres hablan ratcatcher negation

O strange part one no two (enjoys itself)
crossed out jobs in the development package

is the disappearance near?
Lima very poor

things were tight but could have been ponies
gourd tree inferno dawn

Gun Show

The earliest writing in Golden City
left turn signal sensors
                        trafficking
in Variegated Solomon's Seal, Fountain Bamboo,
Black Mondo Grass,
                    creeping lily grass
in the lowland flats, intertidal.

It is not the negation but the magic of juju
and the US is no longer
and will not ever be again
the major interlocutor of countries in the region.

"So what? It's just paper," said top
        United States, "which I have more than other
things that seem to exist" —

                        bombed-out shell of a cluster —

"I am the immortal monkey king
for the twilight throat-cutting."

From the Kola Peninsula to Lake Baikal

Dear Cry(o!)sphere,
                    Hadid Jatou
refined an Expo
Centenario—

big linea on Ntsikana's Bell
Msunduza broke in the background
(beach of a littoral zone,
white caps between here and there),
but, man, I think that's the stage.
"Salaam aleikum," the battleships said as into
the lo-fi potato chip of a Schumann record.
The late shift dranks night vision fire.

On the Path

Cut shin

the question   committed

stereophonically after
this AK.

Le *got my razor.*
Been hard to see   most of my life in Whittier

I work their party tonight

Mi hombre es Vector Year Reroute

pines of Ise conflated with Sumiyoshi

in the snowfall forested port   latch
500 instruments for the tour

a specialist called *cinema before the beginning of film*

it was in the Pacific

marches for a new *kata*

tonged to a cask. "No dinero."

Flesh-Colored Shirt

Lime in the skiey mouth
-ed thyme drawers
the tiger shark rode,
right away do

kiss me, hate.
Strung out do it to it.
What I tell you,
politics receding,

in partibus infidelium
with Mr.-Douglas-Dragoon-
Cosmographia-Universalis-
type moves around the plane.

Fleur de De La Soul

1
At Quicken Loans Arena
an ordinary elevator pours out absinthe,
the brother, donkey, silence,
I salute me, Mary, silver, gone, and *amn't*
leaving folk-tif
                    of late Chihuahuan
official steeps in the waters.

In all the leftover hardware we are flown
for dinner of ground quince with the Katanga government.

2
What was Socialism? Osip Mandelshtam
at a six-inch upright piano.

There were other passages, lineages, don'ts,
attempts to setup numbers
of people's lives and to break apart
winter language from spring punishment.

We set out from
 a huge mute
of sculpture in a way in:

development's brute inconsistency,
the sordid involvement of the military.

Doodles snatch the loan embankment underneath.

Lumumba Zapata College

Free Poncho, may he not face ICE deportation
here today at Collegio Nueve.

Probably a blended Zapata Lumumba
Facebooking all this shit, computer running hella fan.

"This are an active cantinas," he said.
"Cantinflas," yelled the tweeker grom.

System moderator, hello? I have a legion,

whistles a good alert system.

Ya llegamos al campo de la batalla con botnet.

Homelessness politicized
last night late summer on a Santa Cruz farm:

what will the land mean mad farmed
singing like the future Lauryn Hill?

A tuberous, fennel infused sofrito —
I don't have seen my critics.

Gloriae

Rewire
the system to blow
thick with bells / different lineage systems
ancestors gather

try to make
something don't

I think it will be like
—
people will be all like

III.

Make a Problem

Will have to be consist of…
Then came days of cacophonous echo chamber technique
I want to be a bank artist…
at dawn, like the skin of a herpes…
he doesn't have a role, he's a late night shopper

Still Dirty (Subclip)

My Kevlar's in Salinas with Shelley's
concussion grenades
and robot fuck-toy 3D visualizers.
De Stijl dirty, vodka
salad dressing. It's a Thai film. I see.
Opens with drug dealing, people stealing,
that port footage Sippy killt.
Clip after we clip, homie, full tilt,
Immanuel Ballerstein,
                    Blade at Satan's bog
just doing my thing invisible style.
Raoul Coutard on the farewell pan through container canyon.
Chantenay carrots like a fulgurant amalgam of hard drives.

How to Win a Strike (the Phantom Menace)

The room looked like Tampa
in the pool with the blizzards when they
put the music on. No motions.
A tonic in page display tufts,
call me switch-foot, a check away from homeless.
You get there. Intentional.

We ate tacos people,
running like this drum kit

storms in and birds walkout—
cormorants, and the white wash storm-surge
caterpillars along in the wind-driven
terrestrial zag, mercury's
                              wooded
and stochastic cladistics—
bird-human,
                    whale-bat—
          of an

incomplete spectrum, vile, no food

binoculars in the sea bed

down by the flood
                        control channel

                and freeway
        overpass,
                                like a pongid
in the Morrissey wars.

Curtain Design for Victory over the Sun

My observation are as follows: still dirty
"in the wisdom" that is constructivist
red theatre pieces, bike gloves all
like a mashed crop of dyed hair,
a bad crop this year.

We started the play at once:
An Enemy of the People.
A Buddha of lapidary contrition enters,
hospice, tears, *La Clemenza di Tito* interlude

rolled in tulips of decisive consequence.

Sprezzatura. Our row
throws that cosmic scratch,
apotropaic, scalene
back to the corner pocket
angle on the hustle—

"Live at the Paradox."

What is the Car Movement Like?

Not for these shits, no.
Sorta torn, a baby Aloha,
the supernatural J & J Beeper
King's dual use industrial coyote
of where it was ginger
and garlic and chiles. Zone.

Transition is itself the fist.
Marteldood all up in this *For Ever Godard,*
chicken tikka ma-yesterday people making
desert night journey
through the glockenspiel-lapsing wave
like icy sheets of car insurance.
We've been having hella dog bone soup.

Yours Truly,
Souleymane

Star Nemesis

the central ore in the slum-ified
takeoff's footgear full of radio—

       bad love

in an edgy,
          scrofulous stereo,
which musicked the tramways, the bus
route sparky distance as western town
edge of Chengdu, sundown,
               light storm off
branch
      los coyotes

Vigilantopolis

Vacancy of a great time becomes shame
    Buddy Collette, Gram, Carol, Wayne
    Collett, character known as friend
of antithetical predication
   VDL Research House no. 2 form
   of the old clothes

      Spokescouncil,
    for some reason it stuck
        the page class suffix on every article
   that's arrived at through the table of contents
grande peur increment of 5k like time
    scorched a single minimall then Luther

Tombs Called Mathilde

1
In the beginning the crop surplus
assuages the jobless.
Fire deranges vehicles
completed enough to be unfinished.

The guitar Walmart is
a girl and a gun is.
The republic is
isthmuses

to invade to watch Nepal
for Carmencita.

The girl called
that thinks I'm plenty and dead.

2
All of us are none
the night
just these peaches
aren't a slum: Greece,
Polartec fleece—

backyards.

Linati Schema (feat. Laetitia Sadier)

Finally a passage through the breaks deploys the self-protective rhetoric of an innovative present, surprise buoyed by sickness. We were somewhere in the dust/ash clouds stirred by paroxysms of a wounded Sunbelt hegemon. I had seen the edge of global shipping's blast radius.

I wrote some songs for a woman leader about a world of new things. Marjah is a citied village in Afghanistan, the site of American-led raids. Gypsy like this. Have I long? "San Leandro don't have it going on like they have it here," she said, taking a break from the dance floor. Like icon.

First line of urbanized unemployment—a classical one: lost access to land as a consequence of the green revolution in agriculture. Some suggestion of war as an unfinished, Hegelian line. Godard example had been a quotation from Dre, which is either intense or whispered. I don't know how Chris Daniels translated it.

These dying-disappearing-becoming-workers / peasants "support" *Breathless*; so Warren G's influence strange, vast anime marathon a friend showed me, some dominant painterly blue when to outstrip thy skiey speed scarce seemed an old problem in the countryside.

These dying-disappearing-becoming-workers-former-peasants "support" Prachanda ("fierce one"), Maoist leader of Nepal where a recently established republic comes after a long armed struggle, the people's movement having displaced a monarchy.

Text mage / part 2 Brecht / a peach's Argonaut

"Personnel-Mart," whispered Chris Chen.

Bassnectar Is Playing Lot D on Friday

He added masks didn't conceal, super-added
a mountain recluse
in stack form necklace of hippotamus teeth.
In the shrine sculpture of Ishan peoples
leopard attacked the antelope doorway,
Moche style, between two snakes
in Eharo mask, at the high point of the year
in the Elema peoples' calendrical divisions—
this was in the western grasslands of windy valley.

Each element ruins struck.
Sartre added, "Is struggle intelligible?"
A *Solo Requiem* sung by Fandajikan Women.
Just blanked on it—there, acendrada
(deep-rooted) tórtola lakes
is the moving process permeating us. Ditties.
Two na'an, amigo, plus amplification
teaches a deadly fighting style.

I love loving you a mouse.
But who are the actual people?

Short Talk About Freud

The unconscious disclosed language,
the asubjective phenomenology:
the blackened page vegetal;
Trotsky's Lenin in the form dream

came up Whittier Narrows
where art workers
practiced rah-rah increasing nihil.

Dis moi la verité. Sick joy,
unified at last, we were the same hair god,

hold hard hurt anyone coming
back this way, foci of origin
fired unexpected political innovations
in every direction.

                A certain cavelike
coolness scorchingly danced
with the French Republic.
Our treasures turned avalanche
express menu items. Tinariwen.

Todos Los Everything

We will persevere on our Near Eastern Tone,
isomorphic to *Woe, Renegade Bull at God, Om*.
Letters are unkind tones, los mummies.
It am *(f)* a certain attunement to left and death.

Shaniqwa

Quark gluon plasma memory
of myth time Mexicali
difficult about a cheesecake,
where taught you how to surf
in *El Grito Del Sol* gardens.

Lee Roye And The Alondras
posterize a dribble-drive ceiling fan all wrinkle-aid
with newer low-lows
out on the avenue against the snatched sunset.
The camera moves back atop
a Brontosaur back
from the possible image stage.
Buconero. Tecuala stop along the way back for
the ultimate Lolita of the Apocalypse.

The Trumpet Blacks

out the most dismantling Miles solo, Isle of Wight
drift alloy out-working it outward—

fossil waters on additional vocals—
the surge in Honolulu murder—

pixilated darkness so late to the money, like Carlos said,
"Da goobernment? 'tis dead to me"—

Streets and I battled some deep make.
Was diffi-Cote-D'Ivoire.

City ensemble: cotton dress, sleeves,
reality completed by thought a shadow of real estate

lute shall cause the lost wonder
terrifying creature singer—

lay hella book on folks who hang out.
The room is snug, Halal.

Please don't go Suzhou River, *Muriel*
the collected Chronoschisms of Julian Gracq

Mountain fire lion bad girl mysterious
stifling natural sex frightens

the calm or phelm sister of Flaherty's Nanook.
J'ai existé. Th. Leningrad, if I lose you in plus pans,

Fallujah, Fallujah, Fallujah

temple music and time ghosts
pour L'Espagne et L'Afrique.

One-armed bandit marginal utility mongoose —
my homeland is grey green

East German apartment blocks
who remember Walter Rodney.

Hoods of z. Dolphin's on switches
straight not giving a fuck about normativity.

Shenyang copper plating factory worker housing
just after the war. The transition to socialism

after the Japanese occupation.
Our horses and cattle are strong

like Genghis Khan in tumultuous love.
(What is romance? My soul like a willow.)

Rastafari, Jah Jah bless.
The conquering lion rules over all.

IV.

Moreno Valley, Trapezoid of Light

"So, Mr… Hilario Logistical,
tell me… why you wanna work here?"

"I don't know, the… unacceptable conditions?"

The Triple-Double Dream of Spring

The only thing that died never
touched his face blinded see
an opaque process Willie
the outer hooded limits
at the monster rally

affirmed the weak
decrepit culture around the radical negative
Rihanna the soil raven warm
the taste the cash transformed the letters
Across the Sirte Basin

province of Libya,
the total petroleum system surveyed
romanticism, quickness of mind—
called in police murder,
these cynics of a lapsed insurgency.

The purple drank settings raw shirt-cocked it hard,
halfway deep in a bottle of Cutty like
a buried, latent, novelistic surrealism
in Cairo's Moqattam slum.
In a crucial battle, the unarmed *Zabbaleen*

faced down the hated *Baltagiya* in
black hoodies medium,
contacted the dead Imam Walid.
Columbia too was a good
place to do business and so was

the abundant intentionality of Red Chongqing.

Pythian

Vortex-Mex go fireball sky
ungrounded commentary Willie
leaves across different platforms
immigrants form our own Norteño band
the fightingest motherfuckers ever
who won't make sense right now
but you're still their comrade
through a series of temp positions
wind-wild nothing Utrecht remember
we flourished there
the scramble for snow
organic composition in the long term grow
friendly fire non-parallel
family recover the bodies
one side secures itself through violence
a counteroffensive against the people
in Los Ojos

Panegyric

I'm kinda pissed some drainbow
stole my Leica at the festival.
Like Free Market Jesus, he was high
on the Tibetan Plateau

when he forced Yolo Loco
to agree to treatment on a cigarette paper
bummed from unvanquishable guerrilla
forces within

the Inland Empire.
They held together much
work from the deepest
diametrically opposed Chinatown technologies,

single-use cities and the party
crew form of petty theft, plus Lopez Cabral's
laconic register of implicit critique—
He got the skinny on developments in North Long Beach.

Garbage Collectors

Superfuck this noise
get the broom and come ashore
public-private ship steel form
of access to the general math molecule
dirt ice water rivulets Solheum Island
the final account of what it is know
political pseudo conviction
lost just once in Africa Regina
Martinez in Veracruz
a place she'd never known
or ever grow accustomed to
She waited to hear from ICE
We came at night to take out her trash
"There were lacks for everything
the most memorable evening of my stay
in the United States," she said.
"Poujadistes? No, they selling
tiger lion clubs which were just now in fashion
in Anurj's dream —
so much more trinkets."

Resource Optimization

In a dismal investment environment
the roots of the changed present's class life —
Little Shanghai on the LA river —
miles of mermaid stories,
the façade street-level shadow of a youth prostitute
with the back alley club's alcoholic tremors.
The masses rise through
video diaries, the cinematic
stage of maquila workers

then so too reactions rise in the incipient
life of social forms,
practical exercise for the militant
automation of the specimen market in port cities.
The Libor-rigged world over-
turns the benign nobility of a general Keith
Alexander. Tag gone from the shirt
in that blue digital daylight on your shoulder the window
sin barras the resolutions of your knot-
ted busy inventions groove
insurgent and everlasting
thunderclap in an exilic girl.
Sippy hadn't thought this one out but he now needed
the epistemological Geiger counter
he'd left behind in New Mexico.
Aligned with struggle but also what the fuck that plane?

Source

The news from Reno was truly disturbing:
contracts on fire in the new factory
inside the deluge zone.
The close knife work on pearls
enacted permanent nullifications:
neo-fascist anger, settler rages
and the resurgent Contras in constantly
vivified presentiments.

The fund of the air was red
and eventually the blood extinguished
the first independent cinema anywhere.

Those who fought it
were no match for the fledgling hyper-reality,
the permanent state of economic mobilization
and ideological agitation.

But it's one life. Got to illegalize.

The Three Wants

Golden Dawn murdered Killah P in *Keratsini*.
Still gotta weed
get that bread with cuts
to social provision and protections,
to private and public sector positions.
But last night they threw Molotovs
at the fascist headquarters and the police.
No one took the handouts from them.
A crush of enemies converged
in the torched-building distance.
Peaches we ate even stones from a bag of fuses.
Peshawar, stone city in untiring history—
where the fugitives glowed thirsty suns.
A species bled preoccupation.
The fire escape and mobbing too
out into the blind cracked
a run out style
Babylon down the block

Dialectic in a Barbaric Bog

A season of seizures in the repo market
never turned the struggles of real people
into subjects to get tenure
a process no witness could observe
Number   figure   star
corium lavas drifted down to earth
extremely safety significant
like three leopards chasing their changing spots
justicia disappears into the brush
counterpoint and cube tradition little lit mag
light upside your head
ache lesson lowers your bottom
Great Bear Rainforest temperate coastal
ecosystem e(cl)xists in the Mojave Dolphy
circles within circles of 8th note phrases
without end Hegel gente
prestemente viva la

Literary Critics Have Confused Aesthetics

with the war-rationed *Eigendynamik*,
with Kreayshawn
in Sean Jean playing ping-pong
after many fireballs out to the left.
Theoretical practice counsels the unknown.
If a manuscript
has the name of the Prophet
on it, you can't simply destroy it.
Best is you put away,
bury it, as with the Dead Sea
Scrolls or the Nag Hamadeh.
Keep them from corruption
and the micro-effects
of economic stagnation and drift on
a student-run type art space.

Poem

The boss's view: you unemployed,
underemployed, surplus people,
who loaf, nap, or sleep, keep everything part
not whole. Joblessness, the necessary remedy.
Disciplined, we return, come
back into the shrinking labor market,
our refabricated wills bent toward
personal achievement.
If we cross their property borders
we violate their immigration laws.
We face dangerous agents
of legal and illegal systems,
cages or cash in the form of pennies-a-day prison wages
in the immigration detention facilities
of Washington State and Arizona's Maricopa County,
the family detention camps in Karnes County, Texas.
If we come out into the streets and break
the advertisements for shopping into
joyous fires, if we strike, that is offer practice
and adage about another place,
a time in which brothers aren't murdered by police,
we deserve batallions groomed in the repression
of Iraqi or Afghani people, skilled
in the abduction, the trampling lifeless of others.

If we want our places in life
we must pay, spend, toil, travel.
And while we must pay in adjustable rates of interest,
they will pay negative real interest themselves,
as their uneasy commodity money snows in
and then crashes, clashes with community,
as with the exploitation of labor power itself.
They say that we must
intoxicate ourselves with stuff packed
in steel shipping boxes,
and when they murder the people of Gaza with high-tech weaponry,
they say they are killing themselves,
homicidal with mania and coincident with targeting coordinates.
They say the free enterprise system will save Mexico
again after the murder of 100,000s more
in the Narco-lords' U.S.-funded wars.
In Iguala, they disappeared 43 *normalistas de Ayotzinapa.*
They say there is nothing we can do about it.

Summer Rains

over her dirt-encrusted hair
like every floor a ground floor
when the place closed Friday
of the intense shelling

things went to the right
and didn't pendulum-swing back anymore
too many of the old trenches uprooted
or abandoned in a historical sense

and this relinquishment results
from an earlier
rightward now night with power
in the postmodern world-system

in San Bernardino, way in Ontario
there's been nothing strong
hot dry wind
but we have a solid foundation

of ancient Romans
Loxosceles reclusa
Icon gives thanks life
the guard took it away smoke

kiss fog thick light plaza assembly
feeling which smashed faces emit
noise-voice of a horse
inter-household food transfer or sharing

the retro future's lo-fi
buried valleys pocahaunted
by a koalacaust staggering
through descending javelins

the military grade
fireworks in our two towns
ah such green
dirty berber drones

started rolled in after
tides unprecedented
neither mediation nor paradox
total conclusive victory

again Los Angeles
pioneered at least one
cultural form
the riot has a learning disability

Skid Row-kyo

What feeling? Bankers' life,
Jeff, The Brotherhood's seven-inch called
Baudrillard Hulme Duende
something hard
washed ashore in the squares.
Mooch Azul played Society Is a Hole

and greatly anticipated the figure —
grasped the impenetrable
discourse of the coal
ceremonies, the spiritual possession
inside the replacement part
sown by marijuaneros in the Sierras.
The many are friendly.

Fuck a Knowledge Economy
they tagged in the Jewelry
District downtown
They refused to give names arrested at the DNC
in 2000 then LA lagged
on strike things vis-à-vis file type
of which it is the art

human remains puddled

in artillery-shell-pocked rubble
smoke like the anti-
cloud forms up from
the hurricane of
copying and pasting
you are lying there in other people's gardens
near Brooklyn Oakland

In the desert passes
outside Qom
it was religious duty to assassinate
members of the regime. That summer—
Arroyos corren—one flaming wobble
of bloody cotton
traced the blast of late December wind.

No puzzle for the detached
moral intelligence, a material of leftover utility—
internet fetish pleased by offending.
Against and instead politicized *askesis*,
nothing but class struggle, which always remains
rough thing without which there is nothing
spiritual, something other than mere booty,
real girls squirt live. Instead confidence,
courage, humor as cunning poetry and poster slogan—
they extend back into the spray bottles of time.

The the back from there [*groans*] [*stomps*]
Baudrillard-Hulme *duende* wired owl
Mooch Azul on various river marsh willows
and reeds, on
post-political scum,
a sheepish boner of orchids,
boca-created thing in
urban riverrun where

totes different DJ Lenguas read
at the Jeff Tagami Memorial.

Da best possible California Prison inmate finder

is knee-high marijuana leaf socks,

burnt and creamy like sex, mirrors or gears
couldn't be all at once

all at the same time together

Viva Salinas River! a buried, latent, free
novelistic surrealism,
daytime crisis service open afterhours

when memory makes die live suffer
bowls packed full of scorpion prison wings

Victorious song of the defeated twenty-three years later
one for Jeff, one for Nate, one for Will

e la nave va...
Made out one time
in a car-full
Skid Row-kyo side alley. Downtown
rarest dice stances
slang banging condos. Capital having
some time ago come back for city centers.
First Alarm keeps
the homeless away from the newspapers.

Hear again a real factory girl.
Was the dialectic in nature
best grasped as
the impenetrable iron triangle
of global production? Lowest possible wage,
worst possible condition,
fastest possible turnaround.
Yo soy hard techno
tagged in Bogotá
during a scene of the bedraggled crew's
seizure of the helm, a remorseless
counterattack, a contradiction
after meaningless commodity serialization went on for too long...

The political problem we lost
stands outside
the language of household communication.
It needs to be affirmed. Riot, burn it to the ground.
Thorniest Rebar y Sweatshirts Gary
weren't born in Los Angeles we beg

your pardon. The casual murderers
stagger, going nowhere they have
no history just genealogies without time.
Here Thucydidean depth.
Thisa exquisite *frijolero*
from the hard hit hectares.
Rural desertification's
vegetables relocated across the sea,
another marsh estuary

scattered words
for the film, the final
descent into correspondence
where nothing dies, nothing wanes,
the Malian singer's
concentration remains unbroken. Then all the waves
of structural adjustment. All this time there'd been
that zero rates, QE, and positive earnings trifecta —
but here now a Houston-type reckoning —
everyone shutting down the block —
slabs banging...

Like a Storm System of Post-QE Emerging Market Bubbles

Hungry,
rushing at you like a wall of pure negation,
the new cassette from Stone Age Hunters.
What should it be called? Meat Market
pit we can go in like fisherman
scream of the pig contamination
the horror of violation
the artifacts of a nation open
up the government
serve the citizens domination
surplus value exploitation
the artifacts of the new
archive sensibility come down
before they can bone
the fallen revolutionaries are immortal
fearless they faced down the upward redistributionists